PREPARATORY BOOK

A DOZEN A DAY

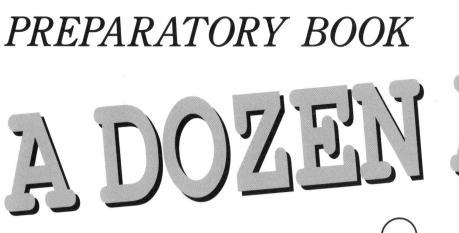

Technical Exercises
FOR THE PIANO
to be done each day
BEFORE practicing

by

Edna-Mae Burnam

ISBN 978-0-87718-024-1

EXCLUSIVELY DISTRIBUTED BY

HAL•LEONARD®
CORPORATION
7777 W. BLUEMOUND RD. P.O. BOX 13819
MILWAUKEE, WISCONSIN 53213

Visit Hal Leonard Online at
www.halleonard.com

A DOZEN A DAY

Many people do exercises every morning before they go to work.

Likewise — we should give our fingers exercises every day BEFORE we begin our practicing.

The purpose of this book is to help develop strong hands and flexible fingers.

Do not try to learn the entire first dozen exercises the first week you study this book! Just learn two or three exercises, and do them each day *before* practicing. When these are mastered, add another, then another, and keep adding until the twelve can be played perfectly.

When the first dozen — or Group I — has been mastered and perfected, Group II may be introduced in the same manner, and so on for the other Groups.

Many of these exercises may be transposed to different Keys. In fact, this should be encouraged.

EDNA-MAE BURNAM

INDEX

To Chris and Billy

Group I

1. Walking

2. Running

6

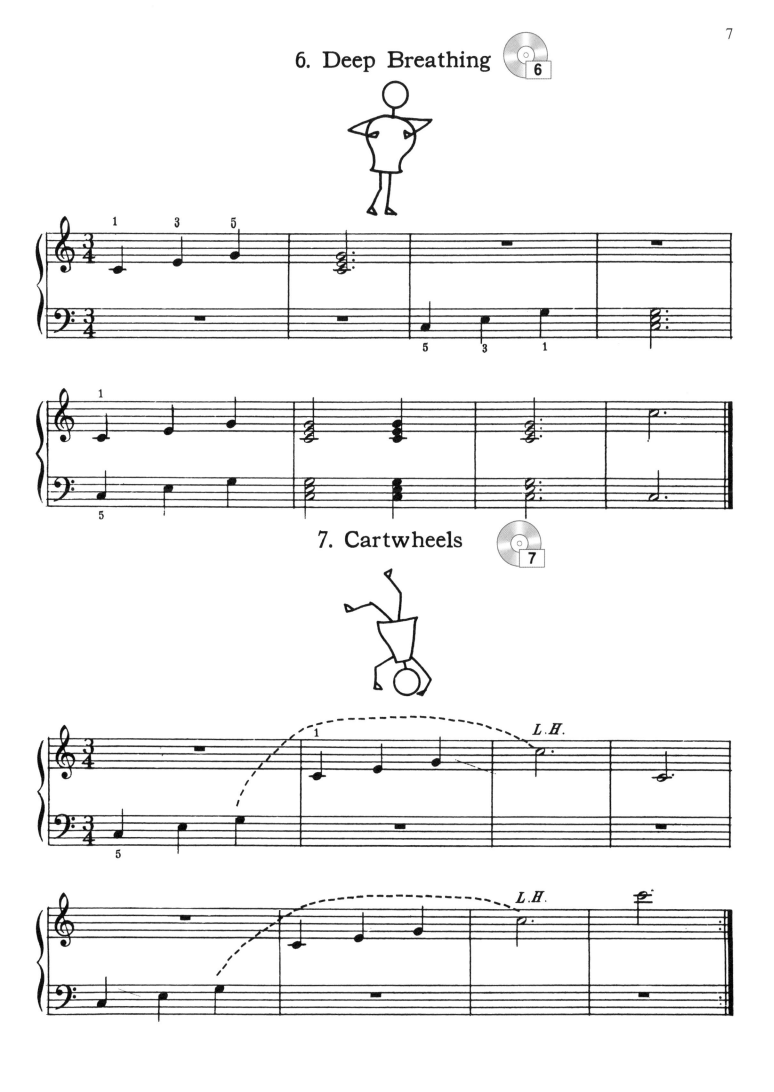

6. Deep Breathing

7. Cartwheels

Group II

1. Stretching

2. Tiptoe Running

3. Jumping Off The Front Porch Steps

4. Climbing Up A Ladder

5. Going Down A Ladder

6. Jumping Like A Frog

7. Hanging From Bar by Right Hand

11

13

Group III

4. Skipping

5. Jumping Rope (Slow, and "Red Pepper")

6. Rocking

7. Round And Round In A Swing

8. Jump The River

9. Climbing

10. Ping Pong

11. Sitting Up and Lying Down

12. Fit As A Fiddle and Ready To Go

Fit   as   a   fid - dle,   Ex - er - cise my fin - gers ev -'ry   day;

Fit   as   a   fid - dle,   Ex - er - cise will make my fin - gers   play.

Group IV

1. Deep Breathing

2. Walking On A Sunny, Then A Cloudy Day

Sunny day

Cloudy day

3. Skipping On A Sunny, Then A Cloudy Day

Sunny day

Cloudy day

4. Cartwheels On A Sunny, Then A Cloudy Day

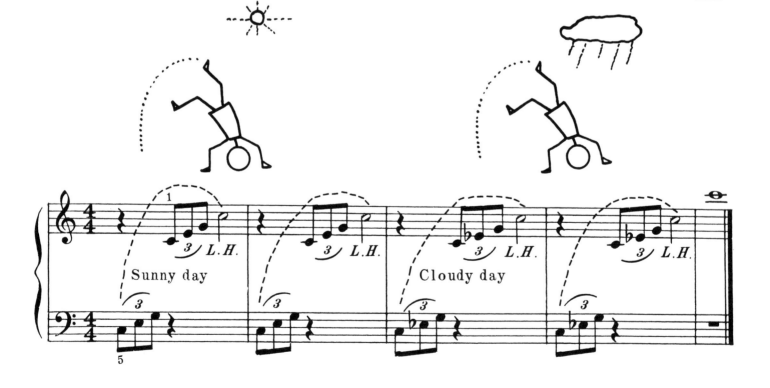

Sunny day

Cloudy day

5. Jumping On A Sunny, Then A Cloudy Day

6. Running On A Sunny, Then A Cloudy Day

7. Walking Pigeon-toed

8. Wiggling Toes

9. Teeter-Totter

10. Peeking Between Knees

11. Bouncing A Ball

12. Fit As A Fiddle and Ready To Go

If I do my Doz-en A___ Day, From top to toe, and the mid - dle.

Then I know I'll al - ways___ stay, Just as fit as a fid - dle.

Group V

1. Walking Up A Hill

2. Taking Deep Breaths
While Walking Up A Hill

3. Running Up A Hill

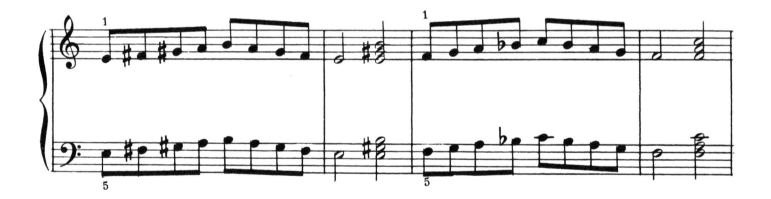

4. Skipping Up A Hill

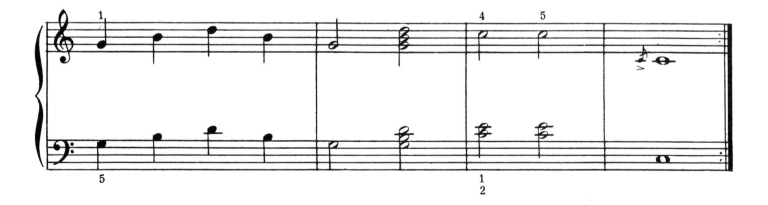

5. Cartwheels Up A Hill

6. Jumping Up A Hill

7. Boxing

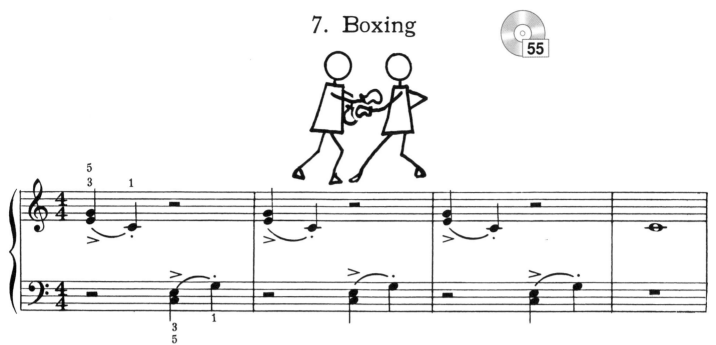

8. Spinning A Big Top

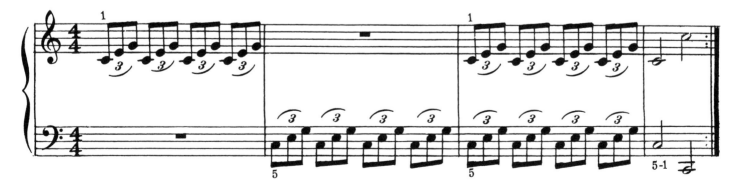

30

9. Rolling A Hoop

10. Raising Arms Up and Up On Toes

Raising arms up

Up on toes

Raising arms up, and up on toes

11. Riding Piggyback

12. Fit As A Fiddle and Ready To Go

Also available:

A DOZEN A DAY SONGBOOKS

The *A Dozen A Day Songbook* series contains wonderful Broadway, movie, and pop hits that may be used as companion pieces to the memorable technique exercises in the *A Dozen A Day* series. The pieces have been arranged to progress gradually, applying concepts and patterns from Edna Mae Burnam's technical exercises whenever possible. Teacher accompaniments and suggested guidelines for use with the original series are also provided. These arrangements are excellent supplements for ANY method and may also be used for sight-reading practice for more advanced students.

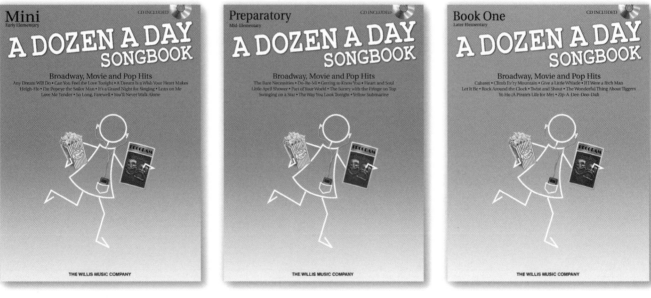

MINI	PREPARATORY	BOOK 1
Early Elementary	**Mid-Elementary**	**Later Elementary**
00416858 Book only	00416859 Book only	00416860 Book only
00416861 Book/CD	00416862 Book/CD	00416863 Book/CD

Go to **www.halleonard.com** to view complete songlists
and see musical examples with our Closer Look feature!

WILLIS MUSIC

EXCLUSIVELY DISTRIBUTED BY
HAL•LEONARD®